Words of Wisdom

Aisha Idris Suleman

BookLeaf Publishing

Presentation by *BookLeaf Publishing*

Web: www.bookleafpub.com

E-mail: info@bookleafpub.com

ISBN : 9789357699433

First edition 2022

DEDICATION

I dedicate this book to my beautiful son, who teaches me something new every day and gives me a true insight of life. I would also like to dedicate this book to my late father (1956 - 2020) yet again, as without his motivation, I would not be where I am today.

I dedicate this book to each and every one of you, as life is full of worthy and unexpected surprises, but I hope some Words Of Wisdom bring positivity and determination to your lives!

ACKNOWLEDGEMENT

I want to express my special thanks of gratitude to all my lovely readers, fans, friends, family and the wider community, who have always stood by me in my writing journey and have made my dream of becoming a unique author come true. I would also like to thank my late father, who taught me to follow my dreams and never give up no matter how long the road.

Most of all, I want to thank BookLeaf Publishing yet again for giving me the golden opportunity to showcase my talent to the world and publishing my third book!

PREFACE

I have always been passionate about motivating and inspiring others, as it provides me with a real sense of satisfaction. As you read through my poems in this book, you will notice how I keep them sweet, short and simple, without making them overly complex for my audience. This can be challenging at times, but the outcome is always rewarding. I see poetry as a way of escaping from our busy schedules and reflecting on ourselves, so we can come back even stronger. This is very important if we want to learn and succeed in life.

Though I enjoy writing on topics and issues that are currently circulating in the world, as well as from my own personal experiences, I also enjoy writing stimulating pieces to give my audience a glimpse of optimism and reinforcement to make every effort to live life fully and freely. We all need some form of support one way or the other, and I feel that a few Words Of Wisdom can change somebody's life dramatically. I have come across people from all walks of life who have expressed how my words inject their lives with positivity and enthusiasm, which is totally amazing!

- Aisha Idris Suleman

Live Every Moment

Live every moment
Life's each component
One after the other
Without fear, just discover
The beauty around you
So blissful and true
Forget the negativity
And explore the liberty
The colours of the rainbow
The sounds of the tornado
Not forgetting droplets of rain
Erasing all the sadness and pain
Giving and receiving love
Watching the clouds up above
Hearing the laughter and joy
Treasuring moments like a toy
Release your inner soul
One that nobody can control
Search for your true self
Get off that rusty shelf!

Never Give Up

Whatever happens, never give up
No matter how empty that cup
Fall, but stand back on your two feet
Regardless of the sweat, burn and beat
Face those obstacles through your journey
Every experience is priceless and worthy
Don’t get put off if you lose a battle
Just let go and shake like a rattle
Behind every face, there are ups and downs
Many beautiful smiles, but equally frowns
Life is too short to hold on to the worse
Just remember, time cannot reverse
So aim high and give yourself challenges
Irrespective of the turbulences and imbalances
Live your life without guilt or fear
Keep your heart and mind clear!

Stand Up High

Stand up high
Don't be shy
Give it a try
Reach the sky
No looking back
Stay on track
Nothing you lack
Full of knack
Exceed your aims
Walk through those flames
Show them your gains
Forget all the pains
Live every dream
Laugh and scream
With every morning's beam
There is hope and esteem
Fulfil your plans
Look at those fans
Clapping their hands
Drumming on the pans
So give it all you got
A very best shot
You will surely succeed
Wherever you lead!

The Storm

Oh dear, what a storm
Though indoors, wrapped up warm
Very strong winds and heavy rain
Causing severe disturbance and pain
The trees are moving side to side
Similar to changing patterns of a tide
Thunder and lightning also striking in
Observing it with joy and a cheeky grin
The violent outbreak heard in every room
Feels like the midst of cheerless gloom
Not allowing it to halt fun to the day
Get on your gears because we will play
Don't let the storm ruin your mood
Maybe dance or eat your favourite food
Wear that smile, regardless of the disruption
Because it is similar to those that expose
corruption!

Captain Sir Tom Moore

Captain Sir Tom Moore
Our idol for motivation
Providing all souls cure
With great goals and action
Second lieutenant in the British Army
Raising money for NHS Charities Together
The end of the line of a final journey
Never left the world to shriek or wither
Knighted by the Queen at Windsor Castle
What great achievements to treasure
Always passionate to fight every battle
Making each and every heart blossom with pleasure
Applause for the most respected gem
He taught us the real meaning of life
Devoid of any destruction and mayhem
Let us follow his footsteps without any strife!

The Duke Of Edinburgh

Let us remember
His Royal Highness
An important member
Of the British Royal Family
The Queen's husband
For seventy three years
Longer than any other history
Of the British monarchy
A multi-talented Prince
With many achievements in life
Patron of almost eight hundred firms
From environment to sports and education
Organising fundraisers for good returns
Taught us many life lessons
Always made great impressions
He was one of a kind
That is so hard to find
With an amazing personality
Generous to the entire society
Fantastic father to his children
Probably one in a billion
Putting the family first
Helping the nation to thrive
His example will help us survive!

The Nation's Capital – London

Such a beautiful city
With a strong committee
Some iconic landmarks
As well as relaxing parks
Take the London Eye
Watching from the sky
How we all connect
Giving every race and religion respect
A home to millions of people
Whether young, old or feeble
From Hackney to Westminster
Married, divorced or a spinster
Supporting Black Lives Matter
By ending the violent scatter
Spreading awareness of the LGBTQ community
Aiming for a lifelong unity
The famous Southbank Centre
One we all want to enter
The heart of London's culture life
Eliminating all the wild strife
Welcoming visitors from around the world
Helping our great city to unfurl
Whether they are tourists or refugees
London will give them the brightest
opportunities
Escaping to the London Zoo

Or applying for a job in Fifth Avenue
There is so much to look forward to
Maybe going up to The Shard for a view
London is where every festival is celebrated
Regardless of background, we are all dedicated
The greatest city to be living and travelling in
So my incredible London, let the good vibes begin!

Here I Come

Here I come
Bringing laughter and fun
To steal some hearts
With love's fiery darts
Putting on a show
Cheering those feeling low
Throwing flowers in the air
Pieces of me to share
Life is so loveable
Love is not saleable
My heart is available
For you all at the table
A new year is approaching
With challenges and goals hoping
It will bring more success and fame
With dedication and strength back to the game
Spreading peace and light
Making your sorrows weep out of sight
Smiling and gazing with joy
Hold on to me like your favourite toy!

The Evening

When the evening kicks in
I wonder where you have been
My heart calling out your name
Take it easy, it is just a game
The moon is shining bright
The stars are giving light
You are not here, but you still are
That sounds just so bizarre
The sky is getting darker
Let me grab my sparker
Read the words as they flash
Before they turn into smoke and ash
Gazing at the sky with desires
Connecting shining objects with wires
A beautiful feeling of calmness
As well as a touch of softness
On the balcony, standing at a height
Watching the evening turn to night
The streets are gradually falling silent
Waiting for another tomorrow to be vibrant!

Spreading Joy

Spreading joy and giving love
I am that beautiful dove
Giving everyone a piece
Without any contract or lease
Spending time with everyone
Just want to have good fun
Without any stress, hassle or fear
Always be happy and cheer
Being frisky regardless of the situation
Spreading peace across the nation
Helping those that are genuinely in need
Donating money for essentials or to feed
My name on every person’s mind and lips
My presence is right at your fingertips
Whether through poems, social media or in
person
I will always be there and everywhere, that is
certain!

Be Yourself

It is always best to be yourself
Even if things are falling off the shelf
There is no need to hide your character
Or act similar to a big end barrister
Be happy with who you are
Because you are a beautiful shining star
Don't change yourself for anybody
Whether you are tall, average or tubby
People will love you for your honesty
And being confident with some modesty
Does not matter how much you achieve
Be truthful for people to like and believe
Never make people feel lower in rank
Take a few minutes out of life and thank
All those lovely and caring individuals around
you
Who motivate, inspire and get your days
through!

A Walk Outside

Waking up before the dawn
Getting those trainers on
Making the move outside
Join in for an adventure and ride
Grass swaying side to side
The ducks have nowhere to hide
The fountain spraying water over a distance
What a beautiful view and existence
Buses and cars driving by
White clouds covering the gorgeous sky
A mixture of tunes in my ears
The beauty of nature as it appears
The birds spreading their wings
With a thousand unique encolourings
Little insects feeding on green plant
While the dogs have raised a joyful chant
Children running and playing
Older people at the bus stop waiting
The wind brushing against my delicate skin
What an exquisite scene to be in
Taking my time to explore
I am craving so much more
The passion to remain outdoors
Forget work and house chores!

Time is Ticking

The time is ticking
Quickly do the picking
So much on that list
Can shroud in the mist
Make use of the time
Go that extra mile and climb
No ending to definitive success
Just the green button to press
Hold on tight and firmly
And try not to worry
Learning new skills or hobbies
It will be part of many stories
Time will not reverse
Things can go from bad to worse
Priorities on list must be done
Regardless of the rain or sun
Time waits for nobody
Not like a still standing tree
It must be tracked wisely
To reach potential exceedingly!

Flavours of Cooking

Cooking is an art
Comes from the heart
No right or wrong
Just be brave and strong
Get out those pots and pans
Play with ingredients using hands
Toss them all in with a smile
Taking care of the diners' lifestyle
Flavours to enhance taste buds
Similar to the ocean floods
Though these can be varied
The ingredients all get married
A variety of dishes to cook
Read Romy Gill or Saliha Ahmed's book
Gaining all the inspiration and creativity
And living with this for infinity
Let those tempting flavours blend
Make those cooking utensils your best friend
Experiment as you go along
With some laughter and your favourite song!

Dance It Out

Let your body groove
As you have nothing to prove
Life is too short to be sad
Or even become mad
No need to sit quietly
You can get up finally
Dance the night away
Like there is no other day
Let your body unwind
Just free your mind
There is no need to worry
Just hang on, what is the hurry?
Release your beautiful soul
As if out of control
Dance like a free bird
That speaks no word!

Life

Life is a game
Without any shame
We have to move on
Before we are gone
Life can be challenging
We may be panicking
There is no way out
Other than to shout
People want to hurt us
And make life a fuss
We have to face it
Or fall into a pit
Let's wake up
And be happy as a pup
There is so much to do
Without feeling so blue
Life is beautiful
If we are dutiful
Make every moment count
To its fullest amount!

Size Does Not Matter

Let me make you feel better
Your size does not matter
Every inch of you is beautiful
No chance of being irrefutable
Don't hide your real beauty
Your sense of a simple duty
Show them what you have
Display those gorgeous calves
No need to feel insecure
If you do, I have the cure
Get those lovely hips moving
Your size will not stop you from roving
From the bottom to the top
You are fine, no need to crop
Now get yourself out there
And shout 'I am perfect' in the air!

Take it Easy

Babe, just take it easy
Feel the wind, so breezy
There is a lot to say
Even after I parted my way
Had no intentions to hurt
But you know it was just a flirt
No hard or serious feelings
We both knew I was leaving
You were never my type
But I was still so hype
Because I love to explore
Did I not tell you before?
Though we were playful
We cannot stick like wool
Want to live up my dreams
You are not one of them it seems
Always bubbly and naughty
Even when I turn forty
Forced relations never work out
Raised my voice without any doubt
Only ever adored you as a friend
So this had to come to an end
You don't know me well enough
Maybe delicate, but also quite tough
You won't understand, probably not your fault
Your mental disorders are placing you on halt

Though we felt rumpy-pumpy once
I utterly found you to be a dunce
You were never in my heart
Very right from the start
Those feelings were always missing
Regardless of the lustful texts and kissing
Always loved my freedom
Whatever the month or season
I cannot change who I am for anyone
So let me enjoy my life and have fun!

Loneliness

Loneliness is a killer
Don’t look in the mirror
There is nobody around
Not a single scream or sound
The room is empty
Even if you count to twenty
No knocking on the door
The owls called out no more
Let me be the colourful fireworks
That gives strength and funny quirks
Killing this loneliness in seconds
Just follow my powerful beckons
Get up and dance to the rhythm
Show them what you have was once hidden
You are no longer the lonely kitten
Because you have just been vaporously bitten!

The Perfect Poet

Writing from my heart
Been like this from the start
No fancy words or phrases
So fans don't fall into mazes
Love to make poems rhyme
Expressions and thoughts that sublime
Usually quite concise and punchy
Reaching different people in every country
Some poems are funny, some intense
Fans realise and start making sense
All coming straight from the soul
Determined to make them into a good whole
Continue being one of my fans
And clapping those lovely hands
My poems will always be like this
With a touch of love and bliss!

www.ingramcontent.com/pod-product-compliance
Lightning Source LLC
Chambersburg PA
CBHW062110140826
49812CB00058B/1212
9789357699433